FOCUS ON NETWORKING

BUILDING BUSINESS THROUGH RELATIONSHIPS

CURATED BY
JULIE PERSHING

FOCUS ON NETWORKING, BUILDING BUSINESS THROUGH RELATIONSHIPS

Copyright © 2019 by Gallivant Press and featured authors.

All rights reserved. No part of this book may be reproduced or transmitted in any form or by any means without written permission from the author.

ISBN 978-1-947894-08-2

Printed in USA

DEDICATION

This book is dedicated to the Entrepreneurs who go out each day with a mission to build something bigger than themselves. Even when the days are long and the times are tough, they don't give up. You will see them early in the morning and late into the night, building their legacy. I hope to meet you someday; after all, we are in this together.

- *Julie Pershing*

TABLE OF CONTENTS

INTRODUCTION 7
NETWORKING CAN HAVE A POSITIVE IMPACT 9
NETWORKING WITH PURPOSE 21
TURN YOUR BUSINESS CARDS INTO CASH 37
PREPARE FOR SUCCESS 49
AMPLIFY YOUR NETWORKING EVENT 59
HOW CAN I ADD VALUE? 69
NETWORKING WITH CONFIDENCE 79
THE POWER OF TWO 91
MAKE CONNECTIONS AND BE A RESOURCE 101
SECRETS OF A NETWORKING NINJA 111
CREATING A NETWORKING MAP 123
ESTABLISH YOURSELF AS A LEADER 133
THE POWER OF PARTNERS 143
FOCUS ON NETWORKING 153

INTRODUCTION

Several years ago, I moved to a new state and really didn't know anyone except my husband. I didn't have a job when I moved, so I wasn't connected with anyone.

I spent a lot of time applying for positions and going to coffee shops to use their Wi-Fi while I searched for work. I found a group on social media designed for women; it was a group to network and get to know each other. Perfect! I could make some new friends in my new city.

I went to my first networking meeting and saw a familiar face! She wasn't anyone I knew personally, but I recognized her from social media. I was so happy to feel like I had a connection with someone. I'm pretty sure I frightened her with my enthusiasm when I introduced myself. She and I are friends to this day, and I like to think she appreciates my enthusiasm now.

Back then, I didn't have my own business, but I have always had an entrepreneurial spirit. Taking the step to go out of my comfort zone and go to the meeting was the beginning of a journey that brought me out of corporate America to start my business and to collaborate on this book.

I hope you will find value in the chapters of this book. The people who have contributed to the book are all great business people and pros at networking. They have a passion about connecting with people and building relationships. I am so fortunate to know them and to have learned something from each of them.

So now, it's time to get started! Use the information in this book to build lasting relationships, grow your business and serve others.

NETWORKING CAN HAVE A POSITIVE IMPACT

"Some people come into our lives and quickly go. Some people stay for a while and move our souls to dance. They awaken us to a new understanding, leave footprints on our hearts, and we are never, ever the same."

- Flavia Weedn

There is another famous poem by an anonymous person who talks about how people come into our lives for different purposes. Some people come into our lives for a reason, some come for a season, and some come for a lifetime.

When someone enters your life, it may be to meet a need you've expressed, provide guidance and support, or offer a solution to a problem. Networking is an opportunity to allow someone to become a positive impact on our lives and our business.

Too often, we attend networking events with the perspective of monetizing an opportunity by meeting others rather than looking at how they could impact our lives and businesses.

I was at a networking event when Tish Times gave me valuable advice about networking. She told me, "Set your intentions before going to a conference or a networking event. Be open to what happens because it does you no good to attend any networking function unless you define your objectives and know why you are there."

I'm glad I followed her advice. Before attending the eWomen Network Conference in Dallas Texas, I set my intention to meet people who would want to share my message about healthy weight loss.

While attending the conference in Dallas, the universe smiled upon me because of a chance meeting with Leslie Akin and Julie Pershing.

At the time I met Leslie and Julie, my book *Discover Your Thinner Self* was a work in process.

Leslie helped to enhance the book's cover and branding my services. I am grateful and blessed I asked two women passing by in the hotel lobby, "Where's a good place to eat?" If I hadn't been open to suggestions, our two-hour meeting would never have happened.

Because of Leslie's keen eye and knowledge of design, I have a great book cover for my weight loss book, *Discover Your Thinner Self*.

James Malinchak, (featured on ABC's TV show, Secret Millionaire), says you never know who you might sit next to, so never judge them by their appearance. Sitting next to me at an eWomen Network chapter meeting was Michael McCauley. Turns out Michael had experience in the health industry and in developing educational curricula.

Michael was genuinely interested in my book, *Discover Your Thinner Self* and asked how he could help share my message. He suggested I prepare an online course for healthy weight reduction based on *Discover Your Thinner Self*. Within a few weeks, my online course went from an idea to reality.

Create Your Thinner Self Online Academy for Successful Weight Reduction became the perfect vehicle to teach behavior modification for sustainable healthy weight loss. The course is a great complement to my book.

Ask ten people what networking means, and you will probably get ten different answers. To be successful at networking, treat it as an opportunity to exchange ideas, enhance your knowledge, and serve others.

FOCUS ON NETWORKING

You never know who you might meet at a networking event that will come into your life for a reason, a season, or a lifetime.

FOCUS ON NETWORKING
SETTING INTENTION

BE PURPOSEFUL

What do I hope to accomplish at this event?

Who am I going to strategically connect with?

FOCUS ON NETWORKING
SETTING INTENTION

BE PURPOSEFUL

What do I hope to accomplish at this event?

Who am I going to strategically connect with?

FOCUS ON NETWORKING
NOTES TO REMEMBER

LEARN MORE ABOUT...

www.createyourthinnerself.com

DAVID MEDANSKY

David Medansky is a retired divorce attorney, an international best-selling author, and trusted authority for successful and healthy weight reduction.

In July 2016, his doctor told him to lose weight or find another physician because he didn't want David dying of a heart attack on his watch. Within four months, Medansky dropped 50 pounds. He wrote about his inspirational weight-reduction journey in his book, Discover Your Thinner Self.

In his newly released second book, If Not Now, When? Reduce Weight–Create a Healthy Lifestyle in 90 Days, David shares his practical, Simple, and inexpensive approach to weight reduction.

NETWORKING WITH PURPOSE

It is an honor to be part of such an amazing collaboration of influencers known for their networking and connecting skills.

As I prayed about how I could be of service to you, I thought of attending networking events and what I wished someone had shared with me when I was starting out.

Being consistent and implementing a new habit can change the outcome of your balance sheet and the direction of your business. My prayer is you will find a golden nugget or two you can take away from my chapter and put into action.

People ask me how I do it all, being a wife, mom, and entrepreneur. Working from rest is key for me and serving from my overflow makes all the difference. You might say to yourself, "What is working from rest?" It can look different for each of us, because what fills us up is different.

God created each of us with our own unique characteristics, and we each need to discover how rest works best for us. For some, rest is being with others or doing a relaxing activity. For the next person, it may mean being alone, spending time with nature, meditating, or praying. Maybe what you need is to kick your feet up and watch a movie. We need to give ourselves time for rejuvenation, and sometimes it may mean being unproductive and learning to rest and relax!

Working from rest allows you to give with energy and joy while serving others. As we abide and rest, it releases us from what is weighing us down and now we are free. Your business and life will look more attractive to others, and in the long run, you will be more profitable both personally and professionally.

I have done a lot of networking for my businesses, different organizations and causes. I am known as a connector because I usually know of someone or I can give you a referral for who or what you are looking for.

Recently, my friend Katie was looking for a bookkeeper/CPA for her business needs. When Katie called me, I had three referrals for her and told her something about each one, the software they specialized in, and what I liked about each person. I could tell her with whom I thought she would build the best connections, based on their hearts, personality, and business values.

I've learned even when I personally may not need someone's service, understanding what they do can come in resourceful later for colleagues or clients.

When I think of networking, I think of building relationships. You can probably find a meeting or event in your area every day of the week. Look at your calendar and decide which events are aligned with your goals.

Research organizations of interest to you. Review your schedule and find the organization or group where you can commit to attending regularly. If you have children, look for events with childcare, over the lunch hour, while your kids are in school, or in the evening.

When you find an organization you want to join, I challenge you to commit to giving them a year. If a year is too long, commit to six months.

Join with the mindset of building relationships. Commit to serving and getting to know the members. Set your mind on building relationships and not selling your product or service right away.

When we date someone, we work on building a relationship—we rarely ask them to marry us in twenty-four hours or a week. Our networking relationships should be the same, getting to know each other and nurturing relationships.

Remember to keep your focus on building relationships. You will build the "like, know, and trust factor" for you and your business. You will find this process to be very productive and lucrative if it's done correctly.

When I am getting to know someone, my goal is to be present. I try to keep in mind the information they are sharing and think of someone I know who might value knowing this person.

Once people get to know who you are, and what you do, they will begin to ask you for your services and start sending people your way. It will be easier for you and no one will feel like they are being verbally vomited on. We know why people come to a networking event—it's because we all want more business.

Top tips on how you can prepare when you find events or organizations you are interested in:

Pre-Event Preparation

1. Look at the guest list and search for who you want to connect with.

Are their clients your ideal customer? Do they sell different products or provide different services your ideal client may need and use? How could you complement each other? Would these professionals make good affiliate partners?

2. Learn who is hosting the event.

3. Find out if there is a sponsor for the event and learn more about them.

4. Research websites or social media pages. You will learn valuable information and come to the event prepared with thoughtful questions.

5. Find out who the speaker is and Google them to learn more about them.

6. Plan on arriving 30 minutes early and set reminders for the event in your calendar.

Once you find a group or event you are interested in, either sign up or call the host/hostess and ask if you can attend the meeting. Calling will give you the opportunity to introduce yourself while giving the host an opportunity to find out more about you, your target market, and which influencers they could introduce you to.

As you are doing your research trying to find the right networking organization or event, call your clients. Find out which professional organizations or associations they belong to. Ask if you can be their guest at the next event. Bring your A-game and wear the shoes or outfit that makes you feel amazing. Your confidence will show!

Ask your clients to introduce you to five of their friends. During these introductions, you will get third-party credibility from your client. And it will give you the opportunity to get a business card to follow up with later.

FOCUS ON NETWORKING

Networking takes time, commitment, and consistency. My style is to join one or two organizations and build solid relationships within the organization.

Networking Follow up

When you meet someone new, remember it could be a power partner, a potential client, or an affiliate. I try to schedule a meeting time right then if possible. If we can't schedule a meeting, I put their business cards in my follow-up envelope.

When I'm networking and receive a business card, I make a note on it: what they were wearing, something about our conversation, the date, and the event where we met. When I send my follow-up "it was nice to meet you" email, I have helpful reminders of when we met. I can share a referral for something they may have needed or schedule a coffee chat to build on the relationship.

When I go to a conference, I like to give myself the first day back to review my notes and follow up on the actions I want to implement.

I have found time blocking a powerful tool for my follow-up after an event. I prefer to block off an hour on the same day as an event to send emails or messages. If you aren't able to block time the same day, I suggest doing this within 24–48 hours of the event.

I block time on my calendar each week on Tuesdays and Thursdays for follow up with the people I meet networking. When I am at an event and can't schedule a meeting, I'll ask which day is better for me to follow up—Tuesday or Thursday?

Another great option is to offer a link to my calendar; they can pick the time which works best for their own schedule. I use an electronic scheduling system called Acuity Scheduling, and it works well for me. What I love is how I can set it up to send an appointment reminder to me and my client. You can use a free or paid version, whichever works best for you in your business.

Being a person of your word is important and shows people they can trust you. This will make you unforgettable and will make a positive difference in your networking efforts.

FOCUS ON NETWORKING GROUPS & ORGANIZATIONS

TYPES OF ORGANIZATIONS WHERE I FIND MY IDEAL AUDIENCE

WHEN AM I AVAILABLE TO ATTEND MEETINGS?

WHAT IS MY BUDGET TO INVEST IN AN ORGANIZATION OR GROUP?

RESEARCH 3 ORGANIZATIONS I AM INTERESTED IN

NAME OF ORGANIZATION:

MEETING DAYS/TIMES:

DUES:

NAME OF ORGANIZATION:

MEETING DAYS/TIMES:

DUES:

NAME OF ORGANIZATION:

MEETING DAYS/TIMES:

DUES:

FOCUS ON NETWORKING GROUPS & ORGANIZATIONS

TYPES OF ORGANIZATIONS WHERE I FIND MY IDEAL AUDIENCE

WHEN AM I AVAILABLE TO ATTEND MEETINGS?

WHAT IS MY BUDGET TO INVEST IN AN ORGANIZATION OR GROUP?

RESEARCH 3 ORGANIZATIONS I AM INTERESTED IN

NAME OF ORGANIZATION:

MEETING DAYS/TIMES:

DUES:

NAME OF ORGANIZATION:

MEETING DAYS/TIMES:

DUES:

NAME OF ORGANIZATION:

MEETING DAYS/TIMES:

DUES:

FOCUS ON NETWORKING
NOTES TO REMEMBER

LEARN MORE ABOUT...

www.melonybuenger.com | melonybuenger@melonybuenger.com

MELONY BUENGER

Motivational Certified Business Coach, Melony Buenger is on a mission to help people produce extraordinary results.

She is an expert in assisting others to develop clarity, direction, and focus. Her clients say she moves them forward, helping them to break through current realities to reach their goals.

Melony specializes in working with ministry leaders and entrepreneurs who want to make an impact in the world with their gifts. Melony challenges and encourages others to live with passion and purpose; to be the leaders they are called to be.

Melony is an impactful national speaker who will have your crowd inspired, motivated and committed to taking action! Her techniques will give you the certainty you can achieve whatever your God-Size Goals are—walking by faith and believing you are unstoppable.

TURN YOUR BUSINESS CARDS INTO CASH

It's 9:00 pm and you are pulling into your driveway after a busy day of business meetings and one final evening networking event. You look in your purse, briefcase, pockets or computer bag and see a plethora of assorted business cards. You remember meeting about half of those people, and you are tired from a long day.

Not sure what to do with those pretty business cards? They seem too nice to throw away and you also know some of them might be good leads, but you just don't know what to do next. I've created an easy system to help you turn those business cards into leads for your business!

Having a system that works smoothly will give you peace of mind so whenever you attend an event you aren't concerned with what to do with the business cards and they won't just be a piece of colorful desk clutter sitting by your computer.

Step 1: One Minute Sort

The first thing to do when you get back from a networking event or business meeting is to sort the cards by the event and put them into a small envelope. Write the name and date of the event you attended on the envelope.

Using an envelope is an easy way to keep track of the following steps and will help you not to lose the cards. Place this in a file marked "business card process." Often you come home in the evening and are too tired to do much more and that's fine.

Step 2: Add to contacts or CRM

The next morning you will begin processing the business cards. Always put time on your calendar for follow-up. Any successful business entrepreneur will tell you the money is in the follow-up!

The first thing you will do is enter them either into your contacts on your computer or, if you use a CRM (Customer Relationship Management) software system, enter them there. Infusionsoft, Contactually, and Insightly are CRM systems you can check into. It doesn't matter how fancy your system is, just do it.

Step 3: Write a Thank You

Most people who come back from a networking event don't write a thank-you note or contact the people they met. I prefer for people to write a handwritten note, but if you are averse to the idea or strapped for time, an email thank-you will do. When writing your thank-you, ask to set up a coffee or lunch meeting or invite them to another networking event if you think they would be interested in attending.

One often misunderstood point when people are networking is that it takes 7–20 "touch points" for someone to remember you. Each time you meet, email, or talk to someone is a touch point. In order for people to want to do business with you, they need to know, like and trust you.

Attending a networking event is your first touch point. Writing a thank-you note is your second touch point. Meeting with them for coffee or lunch is your third point. And as it continues, the trust and likeability factor to do business with you will continue to build too.

Step 4: Connect on Facebook and LinkedIn

Social media is an extremely effective business tool. There are people who don't like to use Facebook or LinkedIn. These systems are being used by so many people; a person is short-changing their business potential by not using them.

We can view Facebook as more social, but again it improves your touch points when you like a post or comment on one. I consider LinkedIn more for business connections and a very helpful tool to use in growing your business connection network.

Step 5: Use Your Phone and Call Them!
As technology has advanced, to pick up the phone and call someone seems obsolete. I know many young people prefer to text rather than call someone even though sending texts back and forth takes up twice the amount of time. Call the person to connect. Ask if they received your email and if they would like to set up a coffee/lunch meeting.

It will save you a lot of time to do this on the phone. It doesn't have to be a long conversation. You will want to mention how much you enjoyed meeting them and are just following up on your note/email about setting up a time to meet. Using the phone is still one of the most effective ways to build a solid connection with someone and is much more personal than email.

The key part of any system is consistent follow-up. This is a critical part of the success of your business. Most people do not follow up after meeting someone at a networking event.

Building a consistent follow-up system with your business cards will differentiate you from your competition and help you stand out as someone who really cares about connecting with you.

There are many different systems you can use to process business cards. Find a way that makes sense to you for what you are doing in your business. Whichever system you decide on, follow it diligently for at least a month and tweak it as needed. Don't give up! You'll thank me later when you can track and find this key business contact.

Visit my website www.stephanieconnects.com for more information on my upcoming events and workshops. Or better yet, call me!

Here's to your networking success!

FOCUS ON NETWORKING
BUSINESS CARD PROCESS

CREATE A PROCESS FOR CONSISTENT FOLLOW-UP

ONE MINUTE SORT

Place cards in an envelope, mark with name and date of event.

PROCESS BUSINESS CARDS

Add cards in One Minute Sort envelope to your contact list or CRM (Customer Relationship Management) program.

WRITE PERSONALIZED NOTES

Write a thank you note or send a message to your new contact. Set up a coffee date or online chat to build the relationship.

CONNECT ON SOCIAL MEDIA

Connect with your new contacts on Facebook and LinkedIn. Send a personalized message when you connect on LinkedIn to remind your new contact where you met.

USE YOUR PHONE

Call or send a text message to follow through on making a time to meet up.

FOLLOW-UP

Choose the methods that work best for you and create a system that makes it easy to consistently follow-up.

FOCUS ON NETWORKING
NOTES TO REMEMBER

LEARN MORE ABOUT...

www.stephanieconnects.com

STEPHANIE ARNHEIM

Stephanie Arnheim is a people person. So, it may surprise you to learn she is also an introvert.

Being both creative and determined, Stephanie figured out how an introvert can network not only comfortably but profitably.

Stephanie became so comfortable networking she became the Executive Managing Director of the Portland Oregon Chapter of eWomen Network, where she built membership from a few dozen to hundreds of local women entrepreneurs.

What started with coffee chats to give tips to friends and members of her network soon evolved into group workshops and one-to-one coaching.

Stephanie has been invited to speak on networking at many of Portland's most illustrious organizations in the business community.

Have a question or want to explore the possibilities of working together? Let's connect.!

PREPARE FOR SUCCESS

"To be prepared is half the victory."

Miguel de Cervantes

I remember the first time I went to a networking event. The funny thing is, I had no clue what a networking event was, let alone what to expect. If only the invitee had shared valuable information before I walked through the door dressed like I had wallowed in mud.

Every networking event offers a unique experience to connect. The first step is to prepare for your arrival. Ask yourself why you are attending the event and what you expect to achieve by attending.

One of my first networking events was a business breakfast. Other than feasting on great food, I wanted to meet fellow business owners looking for the services I was offering. The greater your focus, the easier it will be for you to reach your target.

Picture this, you are walking into a crystal ballroom to attend an event. You're greeted by a gentleman in a business suit, tie, and cufflinks. As you enter, you realize you didn't get the memo on proper dress and you are wearing cut-off jeans and hiking boots.

How embarrassing. Why know the audience first? Because it will determine how you dress. Events may request professional business attire requiring a suit and tie, other events call for business casual. A sporting event may encourage wearing a jersey.

Dress comfortably. This will keep you relaxed and focused on the event and not on your pinching shoes.

After you determine the audience, research the event. Find the location, best route of travel, and if there is parking available nearby. For a more hassle-free event, I recommend using Uber or Lyft.

Research the date and time of the event and add it to your calendar. Plan enough time to arrive early because your best connections may happen before the event begins.

Bring plenty of business cards and have easy access to them. Sometimes you may only get ten seconds to hand a card. I look at business cards as planting seeds.

PREPARE FOR SUCCESS

Now, this brings up another question. Does your business card convey what you do? I have met individuals who don't bring business cards and write on napkins or a piece of scratch paper. Not having a business card is unprofessional, and your contact information can be easily lost

During the event, you can take the shotgun approach or the sniper approach—hand lots of cards out or just a few. The mission is to leave the networking event with at least ONE person to connect with after the event. I've met some of my best friends at networking events.

Relationships start with finding a common interest and building trust. The sale or referral will come later. If you hang out with someone you are acquainted with, you may miss an opportunity to make a new connection. Be intentional, go after the one new contact, introduce yourself and ask them questions to show an interest in what they do.

Be prepared to communicate what you do in thirty seconds or less. Imagine yourself getting into an elevator and you have a few seconds before you reach your floor. You're standing next to a person you admire (Tony Robbins) and you would love to set up a time for coffee. They say "Hi. What do you do?"

Wouldn't it be nice to say, "My name is_____," and in an interesting way, tell how you help people? Successful people sometimes only need thirty seconds.

One of my pitches is "I am John Knoernschild, the Garden Samurai. I help people overcome the weeds of life and plant a beautiful garden in your heart, soul, and mind. I have owned a landscape company for the last twenty years, and I am also a certified professional coach and consultant." The goal of the thirty-second commercial is to get someone's attention.

Make your pitch stand out. Don't say, I'm a realtor. Say something thought-provoking such as "I have the key to unlock people's dreams." Make your pitch interesting to draw in your audience and leave them wanting to contact you for more information

FOCUS ON NETWORKING
30-SECOND INTRO

WHO AM I? WHAT IS MY BUSINESS?

WHAT IS UNIQUE ABOUT WORKING WITH ME?

HOW DO I HELP PEOPLE? WHAT IS THE TRANSFORMATION?

WHO IS MY IDEAL CLIENT?

PUT IT TOGETHER AND PRACTICE

Be yourself, think of having a conversational tone when you introduce yourself. Your goal is to create interest and make connections.

Practice your 30 second intro and use it at your next event.

FOCUS ON NETWORKING
NOTES TO REMEMBER

LEARN MORE ABOUT...

www.samuraicoaching.com | john@samuraicoaching.com

JOHN KNOERNSCHILD

John Knoernschild is an inspirational speaker, writer, and certified professional coach.

John is the Master Garden Samurai ®, he is an expert at inspiring people to overcome the weeds of life.

Solving communication and business issues, John helps clients set specific action plans to move them from the place they are now to where they desire to go.

John has won many awards in networking, 30-second commercials, and speaking. He and his wife, the love of his life, have been married for 25 years. They have 2 amazing kids and a guard dog.

John encourages you to live in your strengths!

You may also reach John Knoernschild at:
(503) 309-2477 | (971) 350-9310
www.gardensamuraitraining.com

AMPLIFY YOUR NETWORKING EVENT

When you attend a networking event, set a goal to be the most positive person in the room. Be authentic. Bring your best vibration to the room and the event.

Remember, you are where you need to be. If you are nervous, tell yourself I am awesome, and I am where I need to be. As Matt Dillon said, "I am going to choose to not be nervous."

I learned quickly to have a natural, short introductory speech. I tell new people my name and the benefits my business provides. I want to be known as a friendly person.

After an event, I follow up within 24–48 hours with email or perhaps a card if I have an address. I mention it was great to share time with you at the networking event. I also write something personal in the note about our conversation, thank them for their time and let them know they can call me if they ever need to.

I like to write a few words or a note on the back of each business card so when I follow up, I know how I can help, or I may even request they make a note on the back of their card if I am interested in learning more about their business or service. It is also useful to ask how they prefer you contact them after the event is over, cell phone, text, or email. I file business cards by general business type and service and keep them for a year.

I attend one or two meetings to decide if the group culture is a good fit before making a commitment to the group. It takes off the pressure of joining before I am ready and has helped me to refine my ideal group.

We are there to help each other win with the belief of abundance, not competition. Focusing my intent on serving others keeps me in line with my beliefs. I am not there to just get something but to develop relationships and serve. I stay in the mindset of being laser-focused on the event, and I even prefer ongoing training at meetings to learn new things.

I like to arrive early before people break into small groups. I find it much harder to break into a conversation when people have clustered in groups.

I scope out the room and observe for 5–10 minutes if I am unfamiliar with the networking group. I may even research members attending if I know who belongs to the group. I come prepared to discuss current events or local activities.

My goal is to be the most relaxed person in the room, not casual but with super relaxed body language, a smile, and maintaining eye contact. I am ready to find out about the person I converse with. I treat each conversation as if I was a good friend of theirs. Not a buddy, but a good friend.

I walk in with a mindset of how I can serve each person. I prefer to arrive early so I don't feel as if I'm interrupting conversations. I prefer the Givers Gain approach to networking. It works; it's all about you and less about me.

Arrive with the mindset you gain by giving, and not with the mindset of what is in it for me. It's important to switch it up with a mindset of abundance and not scarcity. Live in an abundance mindset.

When people begin an aggressive sales pitch, I share how I love doing business with people I know, like and trust and let them know this is a time I get to find out about them.

One of the essential business rules I follow is establishing relationships, as there will always be someone to buy your widget from. It is important to let them know who I am, so they can choose who to buy from or who to give referrals to.

Always choose to stay when you might want to leave the event. It's those random networking moments you will meet someone and find a common cause and opportunity. My best contacts have been the most spontaneous or last-minute at events when I did not want to spend the extra moment of time.

Sometimes the hardest thing to do is to hear the conversation across the table. I have sometimes just nodded and smiled awkwardly. My latest go-to is to get up and walk over to the person, smile and hand them my card and tell them I would love to chat and hear about them, perhaps over coffee.

FOCUS ON NETWORKING MINDSET

GET INTO THE RIGHT MINDSET FOR NETWORKING

Focus on being positive

Say affirmations: I am where I need to be. I choose not to be nervous. I am awesome!

Relax

Be friendly

Be authentic

Look for connections, seek out conversations

Remember you gain by giving

How can I serve others at the event?

Ask questions, get to know people.

Have fun!

FOCUS ON NETWORKING
NOTES TO REMEMBER

LEARN MORE ABOUT...

www.johncmaxwellgroup.com/audreyclark

AUDREY CLARK

Audrey Clark is a certified coach, teacher, trainer, and speaker.

Audrey's business philosophy is straightforward: Every job is a self-portrait of the person who did it.

Autograph your work with excellence!

With over twenty years of experience in the health industry, her focus has been building strong relationships and cultivating kinship with each person she has served.

Relationships are the highest priority in building a strong foundation and in nurturing an organized and solidly performing leader in the work environment

Great communication starts the relationship and a true "connection". This will propel you to your next level of growth to lead others and yourself.

Be a River and not a Reservoir.

HOW CAN I ADD VALUE?

When you approach networking from the standpoint of *How can I add value*, you will find it opens doors to mutually beneficial relationships.

Networking can be frustrating when you aren't seeing results from the time you spend going to different events. How do you make the most of the short time you have to interact with people? Are you able to bring up your product or service in the conversation?

What happens after the event? Meeting new people without a plan does not develop solid relationships, and it does not help build your business.

Many entrepreneurs hold one-on-one coffee dates, but few people have an organized system for gathering information and using it effectively after the meeting.

I developed a tool called The Resource Notebook and have found it invaluable for following up with referrals and with people I meet at networking events. The Resource Notebook is a guide to asking the right questions in the right way, to allow your prospect to be heard, understood, valued and connected to you. People do business with those they know, like, and trust. Using this format effectively will help you build those relationships.

Once you get to know someone, you can brainstorm ways to help each other and ask for referrals without being pushy or salesy.

Two things to note:
1. The initial conversation is about them.
2. Learn how to refer your prospect and teach them how to refer you in return

Once you know your prospect, you can easily share with them how best to refer you when they meet someone who might be your ideal client. The focus is never on "fixing" someone they meet but supporting them through an introduction to you.

The conversation might sound like this: "I can see you are serious about building your business. May I introduce you to my friend, BJ? She's been in your shoes. She's a single mom, an entrepreneur for over thirty-seven years and knows how to navigate the bumps and hurdles in your pursuit of success. BJ enjoys meeting new people and figuring out fun solutions to help them succeed in business. She would love to meet you and help spread the word about your business. May I share your information with her so she can contact you and set up a coffee date? Would you prefer she calls or emails you?"

People respond when someone listens to them. You are building relationships and trust at the same time. Entrepreneurs who use this technique see results and stand out in the networking community.

I love meeting new people whether face to face or online. When you take the time to get to know someone, you'll learn how to make recommendations authentic and meaningful.

Be the person who goes the extra mile to make sure people feel heard and understood.

Happy networking!

FOCUS ON NETWORKING
ADDING VALUE

HOW DO I HELP PEOPLE GET TO KNOW ME?

HOW DOES MY BUSINESS HELP PEOPLE?

WHO WOULD BE A GOOD REFERRAL FOR MY BUSINESS?

HOW CAN I SUPPORT MY NEW CONNECTIONS?

FOCUS ON NETWORKING
NOTES TO REMEMBER

LEARN MORE ABOUT...

www.popmindset.com

BJ STROMME

BJ Stromme is a Northwest Native with a deep love of the woods and water. Any chance she gets, you will find her hiking or kayaking!

She has been an independent entrepreneur for over thirty-eight years, running two successful businesses.

BJ knows the bumps and hurdles you need to get over to become successful. in her POPMindset business, she coaches entrepreneurs to increase their confidence, enhance reading and communication skills, and network effectively to maximize their efforts.

BJ enjoys personal coaching and creating amazing retreats in beautiful places. She teaches communication skills and provides new ideas, tools, and techniques you can use to cut months - even YEARS off your learning curve.

NETWORKING WITH CONFIDENCE

When most people hear the word networking, they have an immediate reaction. Some shudder, thinking of pushy salespeople who won't leave you alone and won't take no for an answer. Others are network marketers: sometimes pushy, and who won't take no for an answer. One wonders how to keep from being tagged a prospect; the other wonders how to find more prospects.

For a long time, I was the "pushy salesman," and now I am a network marketer. Got fabulous product, need customers. Hungry, frustrated, anxious, trying not to be pushy.

A huge dark angry cloud hovers over me, demanding answers: why? what? when? where? All to the same end. How do I get networking to work for me?

I like to help others. They need this product, this service. Wanting also to make money doing it, and failing yet again, I strive not to grind my teeth and scream as I ask everyone I meet, "Networking is so hard! I'm not confident I can find my way through the murk. Can you help me figure out how this is done?!" (I won't take no for an answer.)

Many things sound good. Insurance, health, gold. Technology, that's the ticket; I have a long background in that. Some are ho-hum. Some are superb products, with exciting benefits. (No one wants a taste. Like pea soup.)

A coaching course blew away the miasma and now I am professionally certified—hey, that's very valuable. Coaching! That's it! Finally, something I can make work! But when I read more about what a coach does, I discover that, though the principles have helped me, I don't want to be a coach. I'm still wandering, lost in the fog.

Perhaps networking is not something I should try to break into. My wife agrees. Don't do it, she says, it's not you. Get a real job.

That does not sit well with me. I want to make money doing something I love and that helps people, not to sit in front of a computer, hours at a stretch, doing the same thing every day. So I begin researching.

How does one network with confidence?

Passion, I am told. Exhibit a passion about what you are selling. Oh, yes, I say, I am very passionate about this. Good, show that. Don't push. (Yay, I never liked that.) But don't take no for an answer. (Nor that.) Have the right elevator speech. (Mine sounds tentative; got to work on that...) Most of all, never quit. (Obviously, I have done that once or twice.)

Nothing works.

Still in a muddle, I stop pushing. I stop "asking for Yes!" No more elevator speech. I just calmly tell people who I am and what I do and quit. Oh, and I have earned a professional certification in coaching. (I don't say I don't want to do that.)

Yet people listen. A ray of sunlight appears over the horizon.

Why?

Because I am not pushy? No.

Because I have discovered how to ask better questions? (Every good coach learns to.) No, but now dim shapes begin to appear through the smog.

Because I am certified? No, but the mist is becoming more rarefied.

I begin attending a coaching Meetup group. I meet other coaches. Each has a particular niche.

Do I need a niche? That's not it, either.

One day, at the Meetup, a speaker named Robert had us do a little exercise. Turn to your neighbor, he said, and talk about your strengths, those things you are good at.

Afterward, he asked, "What did you feel like as you talked about your strengths?" Answers varied but were spread along the spectrum of awkward, uncomfortable, even eerie. It seemed like bragging. I squirmed as I did it. To me, it felt a lot like those frustrating sales conversations. Here is my product; this is what I do well.

Now, said Robert, how did it feel to have someone talk about their strengths? Now, almost everyone said the same things: interesting, fascinating, I was curious, the time was over too soon. The evaluation was almost universally positive. Not just a little. People were hooked; they did not want to stop listening. It was hard to cut it off.

I know what I am strong in. Do I want to do that? I could. After all, I'm very good at it.

The haze is almost burned away.

It has to do with the way I say it... At last! Blue sky!

"I am strong in this."

Aha! In the light of day, I saw that the answer I'd been desperately seeking was there all along.

What must you have to network with confidence?

Confidence.

I thought of something I knew how to do and do well. It was not what I had been hoping, a powerful product that would make me a lot of money in no time at all. That is just a vapor. But I knew—there's that confidence again—this would work, and I knew I would find clients, paying clients. We would need a place to meet; I would need a place to work on the tasks they would pay me to do.

Confidently, I leased an office. Bought a computer. (With what money? With the money I would soon earn.)

And it worked. Interested clients (with money) showed up.

I stopped saying, "What do I know about networking?" I had learned the secret. Instead, I said to myself, "Now I know, and I will publish an article about it." And here it is.

FOCUS ON NETWORKING
STRENGTH FINDER

TAKE TIME TO REFLECT ON YOUR STRENGTHS

WHAT IS UNIQUE ABOUT ME?

WHAT MAKES ME HAPPY?

WHAT AM I GOOD AT?

WHAT ARE MY STRONG POINTS?

WHAT IS MY BIG DREAM FOR MY BUSINESS?

FOCUS ON NETWORKING
NOTES TO REMEMBER

LEARN MORE ABOUT...

www.reifypress.com | info@reifypress.com

ROGER SHIPMAN

Roger Shipman, CPC, is a certified professional coach, author, and editor-in-chief of Reify Press, a Christian publisher.

Roger has a bachelor's degree (and 40-year career) in software engineering, along with technical writing and editing.

Roger has fourteen siblings, has been married 31 years to a wonderful woman, and has eight daughters, a son, and four grandsons.

THE POWER OF TWO

How many times have you purchased a product or service based solely on a review or testimonial? Chances are, you've done it many times. With Amazon, the world's largest retailer, product reviews are a key factor in a consumer's decision to click the buy button. It works the same way when communicating in person at networking events. My "Power of Two" method capitalizes on the impact made by combining word of mouth and raving reviews.

Step 1: Find Your Power Partner

For the Power of Two to work, you need to enlist a buddy. Your power partner must be in a different industry than your business. For example, for many years I owned a web development and marketing company. My power partner Jacqueline owns a professional matchmaking agency. These are two very different industries.

Do you know of someone who is a successful businessperson in a different industry than yours? Think of this person as your power partner as you imagine the following scenario.

Step 2: Know Your Key Points

Make a list of key points you would want someone to know about you. Your power partner needs to do the same.

If you are friends, like Jacqueline the matchmaker and I, you may already know their successes. For myself, I created hundreds of websites and achieved the top Google rankings for my clients. For Jacqueline, she has matched many people together resulting in lots of marriages because of her matchmaking services.

Step 3: Listen for Cues

Keep your partner's successes in mind while networking, always be listening. Ask open-ended questions. People like to talk, so let them talk.

Since I know Jacqueline's ideal clients are singles, I would identify opportunities when I might connect with a single or even someone who knows a single. Jacqueline would watch for business people looking for more leads or support with their online marketing. Keep your ear out for these cues while networking.

Step 4: Connect the Lead to Your Partner

When you are out networking and you come across a person who is a potential contact for your power partner, get excited!

When I discover someone who is single, I'll say something like: "Oh my gosh, you have to meet my friend Jacqueline, she is a professional matchmaker, she has matched tons of people resulting in lots of marriages through those matches."

When Jacqueline discovers someone is needing a web marketing professional would do the same: "You need to talk to my friend Michelle Brubaker; she has ranked lots of websites on the front page of Google!"

Next, point out your power partner to the new connection. If possible, call your power partner over to meet the new person, or walk with them to your power partner for a personal introduction.

Step 5: Raving Review Introduction

When connecting the new prospect to your power partner, introduce the two to each other and repeat the key points.

"_ (Lead name) _, this is Jacqueline Nichols, she is a professional matchmaker and has matched tons of people, resulting in lots of successful marriages from her matchmaking."

"Jacqueline, this is _ (lead name, business, something you discovered about them) _."

They shake hands, have their discussion, and exchange business cards.

Compare this method to just handing out business cards and you will have more success in your connections. I've had people hurriedly walk around and hand out as many business cards as they can at an event. How personal is that?

Success isn't in the volume of leads, it's in the quality of the lead. My Power of Two method connects you with those quality leads.

I challenge you to get started with the Power of Two. Find your power partner, know the key points, listen for cues and connect quality leads with your partner at your next networking event!

FOCUS ON NETWORKING
THE POWER OF TWO

CHOOSING A GREAT POWER OF TWO PARTNER

WHO WOULD BE A GOOD POWER OF TWO PARTNER ?

WHAT ARE KEY POINTS I WANT MY PARTNER TO SHARE

WHAT ARE KEY POINTS TO SHARE ABOUT MY PARTNER?

WHO IS A GOOD REFERRAL FOR MY POWER OF TWO PARTNER?

FOCUS ON NETWORKING
NOTES TO REMEMBER

LEARN MORE ABOUT...

https://michellebrubaker.com/

MICHELLE BRUBAKER

Michelle Brubaker is an internet entrepreneur, best-selling author, and speaker.

Michelle is a well respected professional and keynote speaker at business and networking events in Oregon, Washington, and California.

Michelle is a contract trainer and instructor for 6 local community colleges (Portland, Mt. Hood, Chemeketa, Lower Columbia, and Clark Colleges) and an adjunct faculty Community College.

Michelle has created and published over 1,000 books, including 10 best-sellers and has sold over 12,000 books on Amazon.

Michelle coaches people from across the U.S., Canada, and the U.K. how to market and sell online. She has also hosted over 70 live workshops and seminars for local area entrepreneurs.

MAKE CONNECTIONS AND BE A RESOURCE

When you are an entrepreneur, everywhere you go and everything you do is networking. People are always watching you, monitoring your appearance and behavior. You and your passion for your business show up wherever you are. When you love what you do, it shines from within.

The energy you bring when you walk into a room is important. Focus on being present, being of service and connecting. People are looking for solutions to meet their needs.

Make a connection and be a resource

Networking is comparable to being a good party host. If I host a party, I want to introduce people to each other and give them each one tidbit of information to chat about so I can leave them with something in common. They may be a good fit for doing business together or for referrals. Now they can enjoy an interesting conversation, and I can continue to mingle and welcome guests.

Networking is not limited to attending an organized networking group

When I was in the custom home building business and had a job for a golf course contractor, I was in an office where a co-worker mentioned they were getting ready to build a new home. Our simple conversation led to a contract for a custom home.

While helping at my daughter's school, a parent mentioned their home needed remodeling. Our conversation led to a contract. A few years later, the connection we made led to a contract for their new custom home.

As a business coach, I meet new clients, and I am referred to new clients simply by engaging in conversation; with a caterer at a dinner party, by talking to someone at happy hour, and by meeting the person seated next to me at a business training. I also meet new clients by attending networking groups, online and offline. My point is you can meet new clients as you go through your day.

How do you show up?

What energy are you bringing? Are you authentic? Know what you offer and how it can help others. Not only a product or a service you offer through your business but what is the advantage of having you take part in this group?

Know what matters most to you. Align with a group that resonates with you. Find a group with shared common interests. Can you see yourself building long-term relationships in this group?

Be prepared to take part

If you join a group, decide and commit. Volunteer where there is a need and offer to help with the group's events.

What can I do to help?

I asked this question right before someone's new office opening and they needed a long table and chairs for their conference room. Funny thing, I had a spare table and chairs for sale!

It's not always about promoting your business, sometimes you may need a reference for a house sitter, or tutor for your child, or a table for your office!

Be clear about what you want

When I am transparent about what I want, amazing things happen.

FOCUS ON NETWORKING

While checking out from a hotel in San Francisco, I had a personal question that had been on my mind. Little did I know, the perfect person with the perfect message was also checking out of the hotel. They were leaving for the airport to head back to the Netherlands, but not before we sat down and they gave me some profound insights I will use for the rest of my life.

Set your intention

Before you walk into the next networking event, can you answer these questions:

Why am I here?
What is my purpose for attending?
What do I hope to accomplish? Set goals.
Is there something I want to learn?
Can I ask people for the best way to gain knowledge?

Have questions prepared ahead of time. Are you working on any exciting projects? Do you have any book recommendations? Is there anyone you think I should meet?

Don't network for the sake of networking only to have a drawer filled with business cards you never look at again. Know why you are attending.

Networking is everywhere we go and everything we do. Be excited about who you are, share your expertise, be present and have fun! When you are having fun, it will attract people to you and you will network successfully!

What else is possible?

FOCUS ON NETWORKING
BE A RESOURCE

BECOMING A GREAT RESOURCE TAKES PRACTICE

Engage in conversations

Ask questions

Be present

Be authentic

Set your intention - why am I here?

Ask yourself "what can I do to help?"

Set goals

_____

_____

_____

_____

_____

_____

_____

FOCUS ON NETWORKING
NOTES TO REMEMBER

LEARN MORE ABOUT...

www.DorisHanger.com

DORIS HANGER

Doris Hanger helps overwhelmed entrepreneurs to GET YOUR SPARK BACK, refocus, and make your business go!

When you are stuck and want to shift your energy, get laser-focused and be more productive, Doris can see your potential. If you are ready to focus on results and figure out the next steps, Doris will help you connect the dots and pull it all together.

SECRETS OF A NETWORKING NINJA

Michael chuckled as I read the message from my fortune cookie, "A smart man knows everything. A wise man knows everyone."

I asked him, "What's so funny?"

He responded, "What you know is important. Who you know matters. But the single most important thing about building a brand, a business, a career, or a life of joy is who trusts you."

Networking is about beginning and sustaining a relationship that leads to trust.

A successful business reflects you and your organization are trusted. Your brand expresses that trust. That result comes from understanding these five secrets:

Secret number 1

It is not about you. It is about who trusts you.

What kind of networker are you? There are two kinds: Relational and Transactional. You've met the transactional kind if you have ever been to a networking event. If you are lucky, you can see them coming from across the room. They interrupt a group speak to them briefly, then thrust papers into the hands of one or more folks and then repeat the action. Rinse and repeat. Rinse and repeat.

They take a chunk out of your group ending the attack with the same unwanted literature, leaving you feeling beaten up and bloodied. They are like sharks that have drifted into a feeding frenzy.

They believe networking is all about them and telling you about their product or service is doing you a favor. They expect you to give them business from this outlandish behavior.

Relational Networkers are a different animal. They are more interested in you and your business. Rather than interrupting they will wait for you to invite them into your group. They ask questions like, "What brings you out to this meeting?" and the inevitable, "What do you do?"

What makes them different is they listen. They stand ready to help you find a person or company who can deliver what you need or has the experience which could help you solve a problem. Or, they may ask if they can refer you to someone they know who might need your capabilities. Your behavior needs to be consistent.

Secret number 2

It is not about you. It is about them.

Do you genuinely listen or are you getting ready for your turn?

It's rehearsal time and we are all subject to it. Too often it is because somewhere along the way we fell into the elevator pitch syndrome. The problem is, it is very much like a commercial, and no matter how well you have memorized it and deliver it—your audience of one experiences it as a commercial.

If I want a commercial, I can watch TV or listen to the radio or look at billboards. If I want to learn about you or your business, I will ask the most common question in North America, "What do you do."

I don't want to hear a commercial.

Secret number 3

It is not about you. They want a conversation, not a commercial.

Are you ready to be memorable and explain what you do in their terms?

Thirty-Second Marketing is what you do to prepare for the conversation. It comprises four components:

Hook 'em – Your hook is how you describe what you do in as few words as possible and make them want to know more. You will know if they are interested by their quizzical facial expressions or a question.

Hooks that work are Networking Ninja, Captain Crunch (a CPA), The Untangler (Money coach who clears up mental money knots), Business Defogger and Accelerator (Management Consultant and Coach).

When I was doing websites I said, "We build websites that make rain."

Hold 'em – Displays your knowledge of their problems. It means you have talked with people who do what they do and discovered the problems which they all seem to have.

Seventy percent or more people will report the same problem. The second problem will be there for ten to twenty percent and the third problem for the rest. Your approach should always begin with the words, "You know how..."

The approach I used to generate website development business was: "You know how once your niece or nephew who built your website has gone off to college, it's hard to get it changed (Problem 1—website needs changes) and the people you've talked to don't seem too concerned with getting it done on your schedule." (Problem 2—lack of customer service on options you tried.)

Pitch 'em – The single most important thing you can say to convince them you can be of help. This always starts with, "Well, what we do . . ."

Continuing our example, "What we do is build your website where you can change all the words and pictures but we will fix it so you can't screw up the navigation."

You won't have to explain the benefits if you put things in their words.

Close 'em – It is not a sales close in the sense you are getting the order or the contract is being signed, but an agreement on when you can sit down together and talk about the work they want to be completed and whether you are comfortable working with each other.

I like to begin this call to action with words like, "Working with you looks like it might be fun . . . for both of us. How quickly would you like to get started? Could we meet in the next few days?"

Secret number 4

It is not about you. It is about a conversation in their terms that builds the trust you need to discuss their problem candidly.

Are you ready to follow up?

There are three things you need to do to assure you get the business:

1. Decide what your next action will be. Even if a meeting is in the next day or two, I will send a thank you note. Handwritten via snail mail if I have an address or via e-mail if I must. (I've seen two handwritten thank-you notes turn into $1.2 Million in new revenue.)

2. Put it on your calendar. Put the contact information for the person and the problem they have where it is easy to retrieve should they call you. There's a vast array of products that can help with this called contact management or sales management software but making good notes in an Outlook file will work for most solo entrepreneurs.

3. When it comes up on the calendar, just do it. (apologies to Nike).

Secret number 5

It is not about you. It is about meeting the expectations of the potential customer or client through timely contacts as promised.

FOCUS ON NETWORKING
SECRETS FOR SUCCESS

NETWORKING SECRETS

It is not about you.
It is about who trusts you.

It is not about you.
It is about them.

It is not about you.
They want a conversation, not a commercial.

It is not about you.
It is about a conversation that builds trust.

It is not about you.
It is about meeting expectations through timely contacts as promised.

FOCUS ON NETWORKING
NOTES TO REMEMBER

LEARN MORE ABOUT...

https://www.networkingninja.com | https://www.jerryfletcher.com

JERRY FLETCHER

Networking Ninja, Jerry Fletcher, has been speaking professionally since 1993.

This former Advertising and PR agency CEO is an expert inbusiness development and practice marketing management.

Jerry's consulting practice is dedicated to building trust-based marketing strategies that make rain for the highest caliber independent professionals and entrepreneurial companies.

CREATING A NETWORKING MAP

Some brains, like mine, love visuals. Images and diagrams can help us understand our inner and outer worlds more clearly. I love lists, but I often get a better insight when information is visual.

Drawing out my network and mapping people into categories has been a powerful way for me to think about my network and decide how to approach networking activities. I use a networking map to diagram my connections.

There are many online tools you can use to create a networking map. My favorite is Mindly, a phone-friendly mind-mapping application. You can choose how you want to organize your map: by location, organization, skills, or passion.

There is no right or wrong categorization; you want to organize people into a map that makes sense to you. You want it to match how your brain thinks about people and your relationships with them. If your network is already large, limit the people you put on your map to the people you consider key connections. You may also want to make several network maps.

Once your network map is complete, look at the general shape of your map. You will see patterns emerging from previous networking efforts. You may see areas in need of development.

Creating a visual representation of your professional connections can be an eye-opener.

Analyzing and Using Your Network Map

Networking events can overwhelm, and a crowded room can be intimidating. Reviewing your network map before attending a function can help decide who you should connect with and what you want to talk about.

Just like other maps, your network map can provide direction on how to approach networking situations. There are three general actions I consider when networking: grow it, develop it and give to it.

Grow it

If your networking map is missing a category, consider attempting to expand your network. Growing activities will produce new clusters on your network map.

For example, I moved to Vancouver, Washington. I am building a new cluster in my networking map—people in my new hometown. My network expands every day just by completing my normal activities. Experiencing a big life change is a great opportunity to grow your network.

Develop it

If your networking map has weak connections in a certain category, concentrate your efforts on developing those connections. Developing a plan of action will help you connect with people in your existing network.

For example, I know a few writers in my local area, and one of my goals this year is to finish drafting a book.

Developing stronger relationships with local writers would support my book writing goal. I'd also hope to support their efforts in return. Expanding your network connections can happen, with intention and action.

Give to it

Networking is often very "me" focused. We seek to meet people who can help us, which is natural but limiting for networking. The support and positive relationships in my network will dissolve if I focus my networking on what I take or get from other people. People will tire of my requests for help or information.

Giving actions keep my network healthy and energy flowing throughout the map, instead of it all coming in towards me at the center.

Examples of giving actions include introducing two people in your network to each other, sharing an online article with someone just because they would find the topic interesting, and publicizing someone else's event to support their work.

If you are not sure where to start, ask someone in your network if they know anyone who needs additional support.

Take the time to create an actual map of your network and review it either quarterly or annually. A network map is a living entity so creating your map is not a one-time activity.

Use the three actions to create your map; grow it, develop it and give to it. Add new connections and plan further steps to develop a strong and healthy network.

FOCUS ON NETWORKING
CREATE A NETWORKING MAP

WHAT DOES A NETWORKING MAP LOOK LIKE?

- GROUP A
- GROUP B
- METRO
- SUBURBS
- ORGANIZATIONS
- LOCATIONS
- COACHES
- NETWORKING MAP
- WELLNESS
- SKILLS
- PASSION
- NON-PROFITS
- SOCIAL MEDIA
- MARKETING
- FINANCES

FOCUS ON NETWORKING
NOTES TO REMEMBER

LEARN MORE ABOUT...

www.JLJCoachingServices.com | info@jljcoachingservices.com

JESSICA LYNN JOHNSON

Jessica is passionate about helping people live a life full of love, confidence, and clarity.

Through coaching, workshops, retreats, and writing she helps people create a greater sense of life-clarity, stronger personal leadership practices, and life management skills.

Her business, JLJ Coaching Services, Ltd. exists to help you create the clarity you need to act and feel supported every step of the way!

Jessica Lynn Johnson, MS, ACC has a Master's degree in Counseling and a Bachelor's in Psychology because of her love for understanding and helping people.

Hudson Institute of Coaching -2011
Credentialed by the International Coaching Federation - 2017

ESTABLISH YOURSELF AS A LEADER

I found a company with a mission that was everything I dreamed of but needed to test what I thought about growing a business. So I jumped on the networking bandwagon and my business increased because I was among like-minded people.

I became a serial networker, attending many networking groups. Women's groups, co-ed groups, breakfast groups, luncheons, after hours, happy hours, and on and on. I packed my evening calendar with networking meetings.

Networking helped me understand how to approach and chat with compatible people. The guests are invested in growing their businesses.

After three years in my new career, I built a terrific team of business partners. I am making a substantial lifetime income part-time, and my outlook on networking has evolved.

I stayed plugged into the best networking groups. The groups where referrals flowed and yielded a profitable return on investment, both in time spent and membership expenses. The strongest groups met once a month. Weekly meetings such as breakfast and lunch sessions can shift into clubs if the members aren't supporting one another.

Trade shows are another way to meet new business people. That's what networking is—looking for those you can associate with and strengthen ties.

Thanks to the wisdom of one of my mentors, Bonni Canary, I've made a habit of setting up a coffee date with someone registered to visit a meeting, either before or after the event. This works out because we're already visiting the same meeting.

I wanted to be even more successful in my business and realized the way to accomplish it was to position myself as a leader. I established and host a networking dinner once a month. This established me as an authority, so while I lift others as I rise, I connect those with needs to people with solutions. Serving others is the key to success.

KATHY MAHER'S GREAT 8 NETWORKING TIPS

1. Show up before the event and volunteer to help.

2. Focus on making three good contacts.

3. Know your next three open time-slots.

4. Schedule at least one coffee date and pick up the tab.

5. Stay until the conclusion to help.

6. Meet new people.

7. Offer a tangible raffle prize, so they reference Your name to the entire group.

8. Follow up with a thank-you note. Either send a text, email or a thank-you card. I keep a box of cards and stamps in my car.

FOCUS ON NETWORKING
NETWORKING TIPS

- Show up before the event and volunteer to help. Helping at an event is a great way to meet people.

- Focus on making three good contacts. What would be the impact of 3 new people In your business?

- Know your open time slots, make it easy to set an appointment with you.

- Schedule at least one coffee date and pick up the tab

- Stay until the conclusion and offer to help. Be known as someone who wants to participate.

- Meet new people. Sit with people you don't know!

- Offer a tangible raffle prize so your name and business are highlighted.

- Follow up with a thank you; send an email, text or mail a thank you card.

FOCUS ON NETWORKING
NOTES TO REMEMBER

LEARN MORE ABOUT...

www.facebook.com/groups/WomenInBusinessNetworking

KATHY MAHER

Kathy Maher is the founder and leader of Women in Business Networking.

Kathy saw the need for a mastermind group for women to grow business relationships.

The group meets monthly for dinner and networking in Portland, Oregon, and Vancouver, Washington.

Women in Business Networking does not have requirements for membership other than being a woman in business.

For more information on Women in Business Networking, please visit my Facebook page.

THE POWER OF PARTNERS

Keda Industries is a Vancouver-based education, consulting and facilitation firm, focusing on real-world solutions for problems businesses face. Everything we do is to create a smarter business for you—a fancy way of saying we help our clients to better understand the road ahead of them and find their best route to success.

The thing is, Keda would not exist if it weren't for the power partnership formed years ago between Kenneth Decauwer and Daniel Vanderkin, independent business owners who had the good fortune of meeting early in their professional careers and forming a strong partnership.

Power partnerships open the door to a vast wealth of potential, and opportunities that otherwise would remain closed. Maxims like Booker T. Washington's "If you want to lift yourself up, lift someone else up," or Steve Jobs' "Great things in business are never done by one person; they're done by a team of people" have been around and regurgitated for years.

They feel like trite platitudes—vague statements from the uber-successful that couldn't have a practical application to the average person. Here's the catch. These quotes, mantras, and advice are promoted for a reason. They're true.

Forming power partnerships in work and life creates an opportunity to step outside oneself and invite new perspectives, abilities, and a "sharing of the load" to ease individual stressors and increase overall efficiency, creativity, and productivity.

Another of these well-known sayings is that "a chain is only as strong as its weakest link." Sure, but what if you are the only link in the chain? You are at once the strongest and the weakest. By adding more links to the chain, you are creating a support system wherein each link supports the others.

When one link is in a weaker position, perhaps through an overload of work, unexpected life changes, or a simple inability to produce, the other links can use their strength to lift it up and turn it back into a strong and sure link.

The strong help carry the weak until they are once again strong enough to lift others, and so on it goes. The key to building this chain is networking.

Networking can be a trying and uncertain road to walk down. Your first steps may feel uncomfortable, with concern for a memorable reception in an impenetrable sea of networkers trying to sell you something.

While this is a potential outcome, our overwhelming experience is that networking groups are a welcoming group of individuals encouraging each other to attain their own ideal of success, happiness, and comfort in life.

There are few resources as plentiful and vital as networking. By rubbing elbows with others going through the same trials and tribulations as you are, you will learn and grow. In addition, you set yourself up to cast a wider net in a more populated pond when fishing for power partners. Were it not for us taking our power partnership out to networking events and rubbing elbows, you would not be reading this now.

Let's conclude with one more classic: "You miss 100% of the shots you don't take." When searching for joy and success in the world, it is not a search to endeavor alone. It's a whole heck of a lot easier if you have more eyes on the search.

Keda urges you to consider those in your life you could power partner with for better networking. This may be a friend or family member, a business associate, someone you admire on social media, in the real world, or someone out there waiting to meet you by happenstance.

The key is understanding we are stronger together. Partner up, and as Pinky and the Brain so eloquently phrased it, "Try to take over the world!"

FOCUS ON NETWORKING POWER PARTNERS

IDENTIFY YOUR POTENTIAL POWER PARTNERS:

Who would I like to partner with?

Would it be...

- Easy
  - Fun
    - Lucrative

How will we work together?

What do they need?	Referrals
What do I need?	Ideas
What is the level of accountabiltiy?	Information

What qualities am I looking for?
- Professionalism
- Level of commitment
- Ethics

FOCUS ON NETWORKING
NOTES TO REMEMBER

LEARN MORE ABOUT...

https://keda.industries/

KENNETH DECAWUER

Kenneth Decawuer teaches business owners how to make more money, save time, and look amazing online.

Kenneth creates smarter businesses through website design, online marketing, and social media training.

DAN VANDERKIN

Daniel Vanderkin and Kenneth Decauwer had the good fortune of meeting early in their professional careers and forming a strong partnership.

We are harboring relationships, person to person, with the goal of creating a stronger future. Our vision is for you to achieve your vision. Together we succeed in a collaborative effort for growth.

Keda Industries is a Vancouver-based education, consulting and facilitation firm, focusing on real-world solutions for problems businesses face..

Smart People Do Smart Things.

FOCUS ON NETWORKING

When I started networking, I had no idea what I needed to do. I originally joined a women's networking group to make friends in the new city I had recently moved to.

Once I joined the group, I found most of the women I met there were entrepreneurs. I thought I was there to meet friends but really; I was there to forge relationships. I just didn't know it yet.

I've always been a note-taker, so when speakers came to our group, I had a notebook and I would take copious notes on whatever topic they were speaking about. Later, when I would look over my notes, I would almost always find good nuggets of information.

After a while, I began to attend other networking groups to see what I could learn from them.

I always knew I was meant to have my own business. I didn't know what it was, but I knew my future wasn't working a corporate job where no one could think out of the box. I don't think they even knew there was life outside the box.

I wanted my own business, and I tried a couple of different multi-level marketing companies. This ended up with me spending money to buy products I didn't necessarily need, but they were great products, so I didn't feel bad about buying them. I found out I wasn't cut out to be a multi-level marketer. I'm a better consumer rather than a person who has a passion for selling a product.

I was still searching for "what I want to be when I grow up" and stumbled upon it by accident. I had been writing all along, but I never thought of it as a business. Crazy, right?

Since I had been networking and building relationships, when I started my own company, I was already in the habit of meeting people and learning how I could serve them.

I found many people who don't know what to do at an event; they aren't sure which events they should attend. And follow-up? Forget it!

I started thinking about how helpful it would be to have a cheat sheet or handbook or *something* to review or read so when I go to an event, I am prepared and can relax and know I am meeting the right people and the right people meet me.

That's where this book came to life. I did some research, mostly just asking people what they found difficult about networking and whether it would be helpful to have a book to refer to, with tips and tricks from people who are successful at networking and business.

My research wasn't super scientific, and I don't have charts, percentages or data to share, but almost every single person I talked to about a networking book said, "Heck, yes, I need that!"

Sometimes jumping at the "heck, yes" is when you begin to see what you should be doing. Other times it will show you what you should *not* be doing, but maybe what it really shows us is we should listen to the "heck, yes" a little more.

What I've learned about networking

A friend (that I met through networking) taught me how often I should network and how many events fit into my schedule while still allowing me to accomplish the activities I need to do to run my business.

Seriously, networking can turn into a full-time career. With so many events out there, you could easily fill up your calendar with an event every single day. Although you meet some amazing people who are interested in your services, it's up to you to decide how much time (and money) you are willing to spend networking.

I've also learned to ask how people prefer to be contacted: by phone, email or text. It's quick and easy to write the word TEXT, or to circle their phone number or email on a business card. Now, I'm not emailing someone who hates email and just wants a friendly text message.

After meeting quite a few people who didn't have business cards, I created and printed a networking card I can give to someone so they can write their information and return it to me. Now I have their details and it makes me look pretty fancy at the same time.

My last piece of advice is to go prepared, with your FOCUS on networking (get it?). Before you attend an event, take a few minutes to find out if there is a speaker. Does their topic interest you, or do you know someone you can invite because it might interest them? Bring business cards if you have them.

Be ready to meet new people and ask questions. Set up a coffee date. Get to know them. Ask if they like text messages. Be enthusiastic when you finally meet the person you know only from social media. Even if it scares you, or them.

I can't wait to meet you!

FOCUS ON NETWORKING
BUILDING RELATIONSHIPS

CONNECTING

NAME:

PHONE:

BIRTHDAY:

EMAIL:

ADDRESS:

WHERE WE MET:

SUPPORTING

WEBSITE:

FACEBOOK:

TWITTER:

LINKEDIN:

OTHER:

FOCUS ON NETWORKING
TAKE-AWAYS

TOP 10 TAKE-AWAYS FROM THIS BOOK:

FOCUS ON NETWORKING
NOTES TO REMEMBER

LEARN MORE ABOUT...

www.gallivantpress.com | hello@gallivantpress.com

JULIE PERSHING

Julie Pershing is a published author, speaker, and the founder of Gallivant Press.

She is passionate about helping people who want to learn how to write and publish a book.

Julie works with speakers, coaches and entrepreneurs helping them to share knowledge and increase their influence and credibility by publishing their books.

Are you ready to tell your story?

For your Free 30-minute consultation:
https://gallivantpress.as.me/

Look for upcoming books in our Focus On...series.
An exciting new book series created for entrepreneurs.

Learn new strategies, develop expertise,
increase knowledge and grow your business!

www.gallivantpress.com

It's time to share your story.

We're here to help you,
every step of the way.

hello@gallivantpress.com
www.gallivantpress.com

www.ingramcontent.com/pod-product-compliance
Lightning Source LLC
Chambersburg PA
CBHW071710020426
42333CB00017B/2210